Citizenship

Making Friends

Cassie Mayer

Heinemann Library
Chicago, Illinois

Designed by Joanna Hinton-Malivoire
Illustrated by Mark Beech
Printed and bound in China by South China Printing Co. Ltd.

11 10
10 9 8 7 6 5 4 3 2

The Library of Congress has cataloged the first edition of this book as follows:
Mayer, Cassie.
  Making friends / Cassie Mayer.
      p. cm. -- (Citizenship)
  Includes bibliographical references and index.
  ISBN 978-1-4034-9488-7 (hc) -- ISBN 978-1-4034-9496-2 (pbk.) 1. Friendship--Juvenile literature. I. Title.
  BF575.F66M295 2007
  177'.62--dc22
                                     2006039375

Contents

A friend is someone you can trust.

Friends have fun together.

You can make friends by ...

asking someone to play with you.

You can make friends by ...

telling someone you like them.

Good friends help each other.

Good friends care for each other.

A good friend ...

takes turns picking a game.

A good friend ...

shares her things.

A good friend ...

listens to his friends.

A good friend ...

says sorry when she is wrong.

It is important to be a good friend.

How can you be a good friend?

Activity

How is this child being a good friend?

Picture Glossary

 **share** to let someone else use what you have; to give someone else a part of what you have

 **take turns** give each person a chance to play something

Index

Note to Parents and Teachers
Each book in this series shows examples of behavior that demonstrate good citizenship. Take time to discuss each illustration and ask children to identify the friendship skills shown. Use the question on page 21 to ask students how they can make new friends.

The text has been chosen with the advice of a literacy expert to enable beginning readers success while reading independently or with moderate support. You can support children's nonfiction literacy skills by helping them use the table of contents, picture glossary, and index.